# Moments
## of
## Treasured Joy

© John and Alison Evans 2006.

John and Alison Evans assert the right to be identified
as the authors of this work.

Typography, editorial services and production
by John Adler Associates/Pomegranate Books, Bristol
www.pomegranatebooks.co.uk

Illustrations are the copyright of Rebecca Lines.

CD Music is the copyright of Adrian P. Lincoln.

Printed in Hong Kong by C & C Offset

The paper used in this book is from sustainably managed forests.

ISBN: 978-0-9553996-0-2
0-9553996-0-2

Published by Convivial Books
19, Holmes Grove, Bristol BS9 4ED

# Moments
of
## Treasured Joy

Alison and John Evans

This book is dedicated to all those
who have brought joy into our lives

# Contents

Preface                                    9

STEP 1: What is Joy?                       11

STEP 2: Noticing Joy                       15

STEP 3: The Senses                         19

STEP 4: Storing the Joy                    29

A Positive Mind-Set                        41

Afterword                                  47

VISUALISATIONS:
To Start the Day                           49
Before Going to Sleep                      51
For When You Feel Low                      53

Acknowledgements                           56

About the Authors...                       57

## Preface

*In the morning the sun will rise*
*The birds will sing*
*And there will be moments of treasured joy*

These lines, which were written by Alison some
years ago, remind us that every day we are surrounded
by pleasurable moments. Most of us can watch the sun rise,
and listen to the birds sing, but what about the many other
moments of joy that we may not be noticing? Life can be
hectic and we rarely take the time to be fully aware of the
small things that bring joy to our lives. In this book we will
share with you our discovery that joyful moments are always
there to be found. We have come to call them our Moments of
Treasured Joy, or TJ Moments.

You can learn to create a memory bank of TJ Moments and to
store them in many ways so that later you will be able to recall
them whenever you wish. You need never forget your moments
of joy and the good feelings they give you.

Your joyful moments, however fleeting, can provide you with
lasting treasure to lift your spirits when you are experiencing
difficult times.

You are encouraged to become more aware of your surroundings by using all the senses to experience your TJ Moments. There is no greater gift to give yourself than noticing and cherishing these occasions.

We hope you enjoy reading this book and collecting your joyful moments. Over time, doing this helps you to be a more joy-full person. You become happier, enjoy life more and can even begin to develop a more positive attitude.

Have fun learning how to recognise and store your own unique experiences of joy, and also using the visualisations to be found on the accompanying CD.

## STEP 1
## What is Joy?

Joy is pure emotion. Sometimes it is so powerful that it can make you want to leap in the air, shout out loud, or weep, often all at the same time. And then again, it can be a fleeting fragment of emotion that our senses barely perceive, but the heart still skips a beat when it occurs. Joy is stronger than mere happiness; joy adds silver and gold to the colour of our lives.

Just for a few minutes, stop reading, put down this book and think about what the word joy means to you. Find a notebook or a piece of paper and write down a simple description of what happens to you when you feel joy.

Friends have described Joy in the following ways:

An inner feeling, an expression of happiness … Awareness of all the beauty around and within me ... Being in nature … a heartfelt connection with God, family and friends … An excitement, passion, something deep inside, a connection … A deep sense of peace, contentment … Inner calm, acceptance … Connecting with the spirit of freedom. Joy is having bubbles welling up inside you.

Experiences that make us feel joyful can be loud and brash, or still and silent. They often take us by surprise, even when we anticipate their arrival. They may not last long, and are often difficult to hold on to, but the memory of them can last a lifetime. As with beauty, it is the beholder who determines what awakens joy in their heart.

You are probably beginning to realise that we love the word joy and the feeling it gives us. John's moments of joy are usually full of energy or sound, the company of others, and discovering how something works.

Pause for an instant and think of some joyful experiences.

Within this book, you will learn how to capture your experiences of joy and re-live them: each of them unique to you, and recognised in your own personal way. These will be your TJ Moments.

It is always easier to recognise joyful moments when life is good, when you feel contented and at peace. At such times, the moments seem to come thick and fast. It is during these times in particular that you need to build up a resource of joyful memories, to be drawn upon when it seems impossible to find any joy in your life – times when you need to refresh your spirits.

What in your life gives you joy? How many different experiences can you recollect?

Think of one time when you felt joy, when it really touched you and filled you with that special feeling. Or think of something really simple that gave you a joyful feeling.

Just about anything can be a TJ Moment, depending on how you look at things. The more you begin to recognise these moments, the more your awareness of them will develop.

Here are a few Moments of Treasured Joy:

- The sun comes out after three days of constant rain.
- After a week of stifling heat, it rains and the garden looks greener and smells fresh.
- Cleaning the bathroom and noticing everything sparkling.
- Hanging a crystal in the window and seeing rainbows as it catches the sun.
- The voice of someone you love on the telephone.
- The first spring flowers peeping up through the ground.
- Completing a piece of work.
- The first bite of a sweet, juicy strawberry.
- Setting a goal and achieving it.

- A stranger returning your smile.
- Jumping into a pile of autumn leaves.
- Making snow angels.
- Going to the dentist and being told, 'Nothing to do this time.'
- Feeling carefree and splashing through puddles in the rain.
- Discovering a joyful memory when you thought there was none.

Almost anything in life can be a TJ Moment, from the most mundane incident to those joyous occasions that you'll always remember. Simply becoming aware of the power of such moments will help you live your life more fully.

## STEP 2
### Noticing Joy

Noticing joy is about being more
aware of everything you do and of
your connection to all that is around you.
Such awareness is at the heart of where joy is to be found.

Have you ever been driving and suddenly reached your
destination without realising it? It can be quite an unnerving
experience, because you suddenly realise that you have been
able to drive a car without being fully aware. This strange
inattention can happen when watching TV or listening to a
conversation whilst at the same time another part of your mind
is deciding what you'll eat for supper. The brain is a wonderful
instrument that allows us all to function in this way, but if we
are not careful we can miss some wonderful moments.

In order to help you notice joy in your life, there are three key
words to remember: Attention, Awareness and Action.

*Attention*: The need to focus on what is happening in the
present moment.

*Awareness*: To be conscious and ready to respond positively to
each and every circumstance.

*Action*: Doing, acting, a thing done.

When you notice something that you really want to remember, something that you are aware fills you with joy, the action will be for you to store it as a TJ Moment.

The secret is in discovering joy in the small things in life. It is all too easy to lead your life in the expectation that at some point, probably in the future, there will be a big event that will change life for the better, for ever. Most people do this at times; it is based on the belief that when there is more money, a bigger house or a better job, then a joyful life will come with it. So much time can be spent waiting for this wonderful thing to happen that the joy to be found in the present moment is missed.

But it's not necessary to wait for the exceptional experiences to bring joy, wonderful though they may be. And they may never come – what a waste of our energy waiting for them! In fact, in this regard, it is better to let the future take care of itself. Remember, *Attention* and *Awareness*; instead of waiting, have some fun discovering how many joyful moments you can recognise each day.

Every day has moments that are the wellsprings of joy, which can be held in your heart and fixed in your mind. All you have to do is to recognise them; and in order to do that you need to be more open to life – to re-awaken the childlike feelings of excitement and wonder you once had.

Have you ever been struck by the way children have this ability to be totally engrossed in something? I (Alison) once saw a little girl down on her hands and knees with her nose nearly touching the earth, staying that way for several minutes. Then she sat up, her face shining with excitement: 'That ant's pulling a bit of leaf that's so big for it.'

The rest of that day she talked repeatedly of her discovery, the joy pouring out of her. When I recall the memory of watching her, I am filled with joy. That was a TJ Moment... and it still is.

As you get older it is easy to forget these childlike feelings. Life gets busier and more complicated. Often the focus becomes fixed more on getting things done and it is easy to forget the need to pay attention to your surroundings. Even at the most pressing of times it is possible to rediscover the beauty that is in front of your eyes. All you need to do is take the time to recognise it. It's not a matter of having to spend hours in silent contemplation, learning to focus on what is going on around you (although that is a discipline which can be helpful); it's a matter of making the most of what is happening right now.

Whenever you realise you are not fully aware of what you are doing, bring yourself back to the present moment and take note of what's happening right now. Notice everything you can about your immediate surroundings. Start learning to live in the present moment. As you develop this ability in the course of this book, you will really start to notice the joyful moments.

Even at very sad times, such as during a bereavement, it is still possible to feel joy. These special moments, together with memories of the good times you spent with your loved one, are a gift.

Once you begin to live with the intention of allowing yourself to become aware of the joy around you, you will find yourself more and more open to the possibilities that occur in life. It is then that you can find and be filled with all that you need to live in a more positive state of mind. It's closer to you than you think!

## STEP 3
### The Senses

The five senses – hearing, sight, smell, taste and touch – are at the heart of building our memories. Biologically speaking, each *sense-ation* connected with a particular experience is stored in the brain and becomes a part of that memory. A recalled memory replays the stored sensations. However, if it were just the signals from our five senses that were being replayed, the memory would seem very flat and boring. The missing element would be emotion; our feelings. Happily, emotions are also stored in our brain, inextricably linked to other sensory data, so that they too can be replayed at the same time. Stored data from the senses are therefore the key to accessing our memories of joy.

Think for a moment of a time you watched the sun set: then recall a favourite song, or other piece of music: now imagine the smell and taste of freshly baked bread, or roasting coffee beans: and finally, recall the feel of your bare feet on soft, warm sand. As you did this, you probably found that, even if you started simply to imagine, to make up, the sensations, they quickly turned to a memory of an actual experience.

19

Don't worry if they didn't; just enjoy the thoughts.

This chapter is about enhancing your ability to experience and re-experience your memories, in particular the very pleasant and important emotion of joy. To achieve this, it helps to understand the part that the senses play in remembering the experiences that give you joy.

The dominant senses used for everyday tasks are sight, sound and the kinaesthetic senses. Taste and smell are used in a secondary role unless choosing or eating food or – would you believe it? – selecting a mate.

Sight, sound, taste and smell need little explanation, but the kinaesthetic sense is more complex, being comprised of two parts.

The first part is known as the external kinaesthetic sense. This gathers information about our external surroundings, what we can touch and what is touching us. It enables us to feel our way in the dark and be aware of the elements on our skin, like wind, rain and the heat from the sun. The second part, our internal kinaesthetic sense, relates to our inner body. It senses the action of muscles and the position of the limbs, helping us to know where every part of our body is in relation to itself and to its environment. Also, it senses our emotions, such as pleasure, anger, pride, love, and of course, joy – all the emotions that, we believe, make us human.

So our senses tell us everything we need to know about what's happening inside and around us.

In recent years it has been discovered that most people have a preferred, or dominant, sense. Most of us tend to use only one or two of our senses to perceive what is happening around us.

It would be helpful at this point to think which particular senses seem dominant for you, and the next few paragraphs will help you to do that.

Do you enjoy reading, looking at pictures or watching TV? Do you tend to remember events pictorially? If so, you are probably visually orientated.

Alternatively, do you prefer listening to the radio or story tapes? When you are learning something, do you like to have it explained to you? If so, you may well be auditorily inclined.

Do you like to find out about things by using your hands, in particular writing notes after you have seen, or heard, some information? Do you sketch or build models to help you understand things better, or love to express yourself in dance or sport? Then you are likely to be more kinaesthetic (external).

Finally, you may use mainly your internal feelings to view the world, responding to your environment and making judgements and decisions about situations according to how you feel about them. In which case, your preferred sense is probably kinaesthetic (internal).

Knowing your preferred sense will help you to understand how you experience the world. Also, your experiences of joy are probably collected using your preferred sense. On the other hand, knowing which are your less dominant senses gives you the opportunity to develop and practise using them. When all the senses are used, a richer and more enjoyable experience will result.

The next time you go out for a walk in the countryside, or stroll along the road to the shops, or even as you relax in your home, notice how many of your senses you are aware of. Then feel the many emotions they arouse in you. We are all different in the way we sense the world around us. If you share an experience with a friend, you might find it interesting to compare the different things you notice.

As your awareness of the senses develops, you will have more vivid experiences of the moments of joy in your life, and this will help you to remember and recall them more easily.

To help you form the memories of your TJ Moments more easily, you may wish to try using a simple three-stage process. Each stage will be explained in greater detail in this and the next chapter.

You will learn how to:

  Break down an experience into its various sensory inputs

  Store the memory permanently in a variety of ways

  Recall those memories instantly.

Breaking down the Experience

Sometimes, experiences are, quite literally, unforgettable. Such events are remembered for a lifetime with no difficulty. As unforgettable experiences are so easy to remember, we shall use one for the purpose of explaining how to break it down into its sensory inputs.

To begin with, I (John) will share with you one of my abiding joyful memories of what happened on a summer afternoon on a small and very beautiful Scottish island. I was on a hike across the island with friends and suddenly became aware of how happy I felt, so I took in my sensations as I walked. Below, I have tried to identify which senses I was using at each part of the experience. After each sensory experience,

I shall add, in brackets, the words visual, auditory, external kinaesthetic or internal kinaesthetic, to show you what I mean.

The sun was shining from behind, so that I could see my own shadow cast in front of me (visual); there was a warm breeze on my face (external kinaesthetic); my body seemed to be working like clockwork, all the muscles in my legs, which were previously aching, had eased up and I felt strong (internal kinaesthetic); my shoulders and back felt relaxed (internal kinaesthetic), bathed as they were in the warmth of the sun (external kinaesthetic).

Walking down a slight incline on the moor, I experienced an intense feeling of joy (internal kinaesthetic). This was characterised by lightness in my chest; my heart literally seemed to leap for joy and I sensed a bubbly, excited feeling in my stomach (all internal kinaesthetic). The sea lay before me, shimmering in the reflected sunlight (visual), with a few small islands standing out against the horizon (visual). My breathing was effortless (internal kinaesthetic). The moor beneath my feet was carpeted with tiny wild orchids and other flowers I could not name (visual). At that point in the walk, my companions and I were silent because we were approaching a spiritual place that demanded our respect, so all that could be heard was the swish of our boots brushing the heather (auditory – in this case mainly the silence). It was a time of treasured joy, and as I noticed and re-noticed every detail, the experience seemed to grow inside me (internal kinaesthetic) and I knew that I would want to return here at will in my mind, even if I never physically visited this beautiful place again.

Noticing my surroundings in such detail did not detract from the pleasure of the moment – it added to it!

With your unique balance of sensory organs and preferred senses, you would probably have sensed that experience in a different way; you may have a keen sense of smell, which I don't have, in which case the scent of the sea, or the peat in the moor, would have been more noticeable to you; the feelings of elation I experienced might have been felt somewhere else in your body – your head, your shoulders, or upper chest perhaps. The important thing would have been that you noticed them.

To help you learn how to become aware of such an experience in your life, try to remember one of your own abiding moments of treasured joy.

Sit somewhere you will not be disturbed. You might find it helpful to close your eyes; you might even like to relax a little. To simplify the process for yourself, as you begin to recall your experience, ask yourself these questions in turn: 'What can I see?' 'What can I hear?' 'What do I feel, both inside me and around me?' 'Can I smell or taste anything?'

Give yourself plenty of time for your memory to respond and notice as much detail as you can.

Having done that, you will have built up an initial recollection of your experience. Even though your eyes might be closed, move them, or your head, to look in another direction in the scene; incline your head to identify any other sounds, just as you might have done on the day. Ask those same questions again, adding, 'Is there anything else?', and wait to see what, if anything, comes up.

You may find that, as you analyse your experience in this way, you will re-live it more vividly and clearly than you ever have before. In fact, your mind probably stored much more information from your senses than you thought it had. As one recalled sensation triggers the memory of another, you will build up an even richer experience than you expected. If this happens, you can now appreciate why it is helpful to use as many of the senses as you have at your disposal. Remember, in your brain all the sensory information stored from that experience is connected; the recalling of just one bit of data, a sight, a sound and so on, can trigger the recall of others. One of them will be the pleasant emotion of joy you felt at the time.

Perhaps you would like to recall other pleasant memories in this way, to practise the method before continuing. As you do so, re-experiencing such events will become natural and effortless.

In the next chapter, you will discover how to store and recall your sensory data in such a way that it improves not only the quality of the memory, but the ease and effectiveness of recalling it. The joy of your original experience will be yours again.

## STEP 4
### Storing the Joy

This chapter is about finding different ways to remember your TJ Moments so that, whenever you wish, you will be able to recall what it was that gave you so much pleasure. In many instances, you will be able to recall the occasion as if you were back in the original moment.

In order to remember TJ Moments easily, and to experience them fully whenever you would like, the way you store them can facilitate their recall. In the last chapter, you learned that careful noting of how you sense an experience can greatly improve the chance of achieving an accurate recall from your memory.

Here are five different ways of memory storage and recall that are suitable for a range of preferred senses. They may be used either on their own, or together.

1. Create a Joy Memory Box

One way of generating a tangible reminder of the joyful moments in your life is to create a box of memories.

♦ Find a box that looks and feels right for you. Because your memories are special, it is important to choose a box that reflects this. You may already have a box at home, or you may wish to buy one. Finding one to which you are particularly drawn can be a TJ Moment in itself.

• Spend some time recollecting joyful times that have occurred in your life, both from years ago and from recent times.

• Think of something you could put into the box that will be a reminder of each joyful occasion. It could be a photograph, a letter, a picture of a flower, a pine cone, a lock of hair, a piece of music, a book; in fact, anything that will bring back the memory for you.

• As you recognise a new TJ Moment, you can put a memento into the box.

• If you want to think about a happy time, or if you are feeling low, open the box and go through the reminders stored there. Give yourself time. Allow yourself to smile and laugh as you recollect everything about those joyful occasions.

2. Keep a TJ Moments Book

Similar to the Memory Box, the book is a place you can record particular joyful moments.

♦ Choose a suitable notebook. As with the box, choose one that you find attractive and easy to use, perhaps one small enough to carry around with you.

♦ As a moment occurs that you really want to store, sketch something, write a word or a sentence about it, or keep a memento to paste into the book. Put down where you are, the date and what it was that you noticed, or anything that helps to reinforce the memory. Include some sensory input, such as a visual description, sounds you heard or scents. Anything that will stimulate the memory can be useful, even if it does not seem obviously connected to the experience.

♦ If you read or hear something that gladdens your heart, write it down with the author's name.

♦ Before you go to sleep, look through your book. This way you will go to sleep with a joyful feeling inside you.

3. Reminding Yourself of Your Joyful Moments

It sounds rather obvious, but the act of remembering a positive experience is helped enormously by going over it in your mind after the event. The more repetitions, the better the memory retention, and it's good to re-experience the pleasure every time.

When something negative happens to you, can you let it go, or do you keep thinking about the incident, replaying it over and over again in your mind? If you do the latter, painful memories can last for a long time. So why not make use of this effect and build lasting memories of the good things that happen? This is how to do it.

♦ When a TJ Moment happens, acknowledge how good it feels and say to yourself, 'I'm going to remember this.'

♦ Take a few seconds to notice as much about it as you can through your senses. Then keep going back to it in your mind, several times during that day, a few times the next day, and then every so often for the next month or so.

♦ Recall it as faithfully as you can each time and enjoy the moment again and again.

Repeatedly recalling the moment over time will implant the experience firmly in your mind.

Using this process in conjunction with your memory book and box helps generate a really powerful memory storage of the event.

Remembering in this way leads naturally to the last way of storing the TJ Moments, that of associating words and gestures with each moment and using them later to trigger an instant recall of the memory.

4. Instant Recall of Your TJ Moments

There are two ways you can store memories so that you can recall them instantly. The first enables all the detail of your experience to be remembered. When practised a few times, it takes only about a minute to do so. The second method stores and recalls just the emotion of joy from an experience and is a much shorter and easier method to use; it takes only a second or so.

For reasons that will become obvious, you may not want to use the longer method every time you experience a TJ Moment, but almost certainly you will use the shorter method every time.

The full technique can be used for all memories though it is particularly suited for the sublime, Aha-type, moments in your life – those you will never want to forget. Because these often happen unexpectedly, probably when you have no access to recording equipment of any kind, this moment gets stored immediately and firmly in your mind. The recall is often so good it is like being there again.

It is unlikely, for instance, that you will ever forget the joyful experience you used for the exercise at the end of the last chapter. You have probably realised that, by remembering the experience in great detail and using as many different senses as you could, an even richer and more pleasurable memory was evoked than you had thought possible. If you could store that full memory in your mind and be able to re-call it instantly in all its vividness, would you like that? I'm sure you would, and here's how you do it.

The essence of the technique is very simple and relies on associating a trigger word and action with the moment you experience. Later, when you wish to recall the scene and your feelings, you simply repeat the word and gesture and the TJ Moment will come flooding back.

In the CD accompanying this book, you will be led through the process, so you don't need to learn anything at this point or be distracted by looking down at the text.

Reading it through first, however, will give you an idea of what to expect. After practising for a while, the process becomes easy to use. Here is the sequence:

a.    Choose a TJ Moment you want to be able to remember and recall vividly – what you saw, what you heard, what you felt (both inside and outside your body – and where physically the feelings were located, i.e. head, chest, stomach etc.) and what you could taste and smell. Allow the experience to build up. Take your time with this so as to enjoy it and re-live the good feeling. At some point the experience will peak, and then fade; you can't stay in a state of euphoria for too long! Get some idea of what it feels like as you approach the peak of the experience. Then come out of the experience and relax.

b.  Take a break and distract yourself for about 30 seconds by thinking about something else, such as 'What's for dinner?'… or look out of the window to see what's happening outside.

c.  Decide on a simple word and gesture you will use to trigger the TJ Moment. The word will normally be said silently, and have some connection with the content of the TJ Moment; and the gesture should be something that is subtle and accurately repeatable, like scratching an ear or your nose, or touching together a thumb and finger. Practise these triggers and you'll soon get the hang of it.

d.  Repeat (a), building up the experience of the TJ Moment in exactly the same way as before. You may even remember more this time, and when you think you are nearly at the peak of the experience, say the trigger word and make the trigger gesture.

e.  Take a break again by thinking of something else, like

'What am I going to wear tomorrow?' Shake your body around; brush yourself down with your hands and get ready to go again.

f.    Practice makes perfect, and between three and six repeats of (d) and (e) should be enough to store the experience firmly in your memory, linked to your unique triggers. Make sure you repeat the gesture trigger as precisely as you can. It will become easier to recall the original experience, and the peak comes upon you more quickly, so be ready with the triggers.

g.    The last step is to test that the process has worked. After the last break, wait a few more moments, then say the trigger word and make the gesture. The TJ Moment will be recalled instantly. When that happens you will know that the process has worked for you.

Congratulations, you are now the proud owner of your TJ Moment and are able to store any TJ Moments in your life as they happen, and recall them in an instant, just when you want.

Every time you store and recall a TJ Moment with this method, you need to think of a unique trigger word and gesture to accompany it, which means you will end up with lots of different triggers to remember. Also, the technique is best used when you are in the moment, with time to spare, as when on the island walk described to you earlier.

If you want simply to collect the emotion of joy, without worrying about any of the details of the experience that produced it, there is another, easier, way to do this. It's explained below.

5. Storing and Recalling the Emotion of Joy

This simple version of the instant recall technique uses the same trigger word and gesture for every TJ Moment. You do not have to think about the details of the experience, or note which senses you are using. When the Moment occurs and the feeling of joy rises up in you, say your joy word and make your joy gesture. That's all you have to do. Over time, as you experience more TJ Moments, collect the feelings of joy on each occasion. You will discover that activating your triggers at any time will make you feel more joyful.

You now have one technique for storing the pure joy in every TJ Moment and another for adding in the detail of the experience. Don't worry about having to decide which method to use. As a rule, always use the quick method first. If you decide later that you'd like to store the detail as well, go back in your mind to the full memory, use the longer sequence described in the previous section (4) and re-store it with a unique trigger word and gesture.

Both methods will become as second nature to you as you use them repeatedly.

All you need now is to wonder when and from where your next Moment of Treasured Joy will come to you. From without or within it will surely arrive to give you pleasure in the moment and many times after. Have fun!

## A Small (but not Insignificant) Health Warning

You may have begun to realise that, as well as collecting joy experiences, you could similarly collect your experiences of courage, confidence, or some other positive state of mind – and so you can. Many people, especially in the business world, use the last two techniques to enhance their performance when, for instance, giving presentations or participating in important meetings. There is, however, a health warning attached to over-using one particular emotional state, the state of feeling energetic. So many of us wish we had more energy, particularly when we are overcome by tiredness, and might think to draw on our moments of treasured energy. Beware! Tiredness is the body's way of saying slow down. If you choose to override that signal too often, your body will strike back sooner or later, with adverse consequences for your health and well-being.

In a similar vein, when you experience emotional pain, like a bereavement or parting, it is not usually appropriate to try to mask the feelings of sadness with a happy or joyful state. Grieving is part of the healing process, and it is not recommended that you use this technique in such situations.

The golden rule is to think very carefully before you choose repeatedly to override the body's natural healing and restorative processes.

## A Positive Mind-Set

With more joy in your life, your whole outlook on the world can begin to change. You will almost certainly become happier, you will begin to enjoy life more and you are likely to develop a more positive frame of mind. A positive mind-set makes it easier to spot the moments of joy – and that's where we came in, learning how to notice the TJ Moments.

It all sounds so easy and straightforward to achieve! So what would stop you doing that, or even wanting to? Sometimes we have found it hard ourselves to summon up the enthusiasm to notice TJ Moments; we can't even be bothered to look for them. Usually this is because we are distracted by negative thoughts and emotions, so in this chapter we want to offer you some suggestions about what to do if this happens to you too.

The three words 'Attention, Awareness and Action' were introduced in Step 2 in the context of becoming more aware of your surroundings.

This chapter emphasises the need for awareness of the type of thinking that stops us enjoying life. We know such thoughts will pass, but often there are lessons to be learned and it is useful to pause just long enough to think what they might be so that you can do something about it.

*When you are feeling low*
Throughout the book we have encouraged you to live in the now, whatever state you are in. So accept the fact that you are feeling low and spend time experiencing that emotion. Try not to beat yourself up about it, and let acceptance be the joyful experience for that day.

If possible, try to maintain part of your awareness of your surroundings in case something of joy comes along, no matter how small. Allow yourself to acknowledge the moment. You will have great encouragement from being able to look back and say, 'I was at my lowest ebb, but I let that beautiful sunset … that smile from a stranger … that funny advert on TV … enter my mind and bring an awareness of joy.'

*When a conflict arises that upsets you.*
Living in the now is having an awareness not just of what is happening around you, but also of what is happening within you.

When you are confronted with a difficult situation, you may discover that you invariably respond in the same way. You may be content with how you behave, or you may not. Noticing that you want to change and wondering how you might behave differently next time is a sure way of living less stressfully. Such thinking is also the hallmark of a positive mind-set. You gain the ability to influence the way you think and behave. Being aware of the way you think is an enormous step towards living a more joy-filled life.

*Say positive things about yourself.*
The words you use to express how you think about yourself, whether they are spoken out loud, or silently in your head, are far more important than you might think. Hearing continual messages of encouragement is really beneficial to your physical and mental health; hearing continual reproachful messages does the opposite and slowly destroys your confidence. Think about what you'd like to hear others say to you, and say it to yourself; be your own cheerleader, and encourage yourself when you are experiencing problems. Changing your language to support yourself is a very important step forward in maintaining your positive mind-set.

*Change your point of view.*
Are you an optimist or a pessimist? Do you tend towards cheerfulness, or do you find yourself complaining a lot? If you are confronted with a situation you would normally be negative about, ask yourself, 'How can I think about this more positively?' For example, when you get up late in the morning, instead of immediately thinking you will be unable to get

everything done that day, could you possibly think instead that the extra sleep will give you more energy to finish all you need to do? Or, when you see some young people demonstrating against the building of a new road through a green field, you might think of them as vandals; but instead, could you respect them for caring so much about the environment?

*Know the limits of your control.*
There are many things in life that make us feel helpless: world events, poverty, illness and crime are just some examples. There are some things you might feel you can do something about, either on your own or with the help of a group of like-minded individuals. But, whilst huge changes have occurred over the years by such involvement, the truth is that no matter how great the personal effort, there are some events and situations over which you will have little or no control. Knowing the difference between what you can and cannot change, accepting this and putting your energies only into the former, is likely to bring you greater joy than a lifetime spent worrying about the latter.

*Judge yourself and others more kindly.*
As you come to enjoy life more and more, you are increasingly likely to judge yourself and others kindly. Even, especially at stressful and difficult times, appreciate yourself more by using

words of encouragement. Tell yourself, 'I'm doing the best I can', 'I'm learning a lot about myself at the moment', and 'I'm doing OK'. By being more respectful of yourself, you will be able to give that same respect to others.

However your day goes, make a commitment to yourself that, before going to sleep, you will focus your mind on something joyful, either by remembering a previous experience or by positively anticipating what joy the next day could bring.

To help you with this, you may wish to have a small card by your bed with a positive affirmation on it. When you wake in the morning, read the card so your first thoughts are ones of joy. You can use the following sayings or write some of your own which are especially meaningful to you.

> Think joy
> Feel joyful
> Spread joy

> I breathe in joy
> I breathe out joy
> I am filled with joy, peace and love

Joy is a simple but profound treasure – and it costs you nothing to experience it.

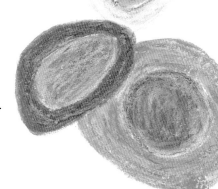

## Afterword

We hope you have enjoyed learning to recognise and capture forever those TJ Moments that were slipping by, often unnoticed. Perhaps this book has reconnected you with an emotion that is often forgotten.

Enter Joy, coming not as an escape from the world, but as a positive force for goodness and sanity.

Joy is free and freely available to anyone who wishes to experience it. Who knows? As you become more joyful, others will begin to notice the change in you and want to experience it for themselves. Your joy will then have rippled out into another's existence, and that too will be a real Moment of Treasured Joy.

## Visualisation to Start the Day

As you wake up, let your mind focus on the day ahead. Give yourself a few moments to think of all the possibilities for joy that this day may bring.

Run through how you anticipate you are going to feel:

The people or sights you will see.
The voices you will hear.
The smell and taste of the food you may eat.
How you will use your hands today.

Let your intention be to find in this day some moments of treasured joy. There is time both to receive and also to give joy.

Awaken your senses to all this day has to offer.
Awaken each part of you to all that you can offer others just by being yourself.
Become aware that as you experience your life in a joyful way, the positive energy you give out will affect each person you meet.

The ripples of joyful energy will spread out like the ripples when a pebble is dropped into a pool of water.

Go into this day alert to everything around you. Recognise all that you can learn from every encounter and experience.

Be still for a moment, and when you are ready get out of bed, stretch and move your shoulders, smile and go on with the day.

## Visualisation before Going to Sleep

To begin with, make sure you are lying comfortably and begin to relax. You may want to close your eyes; it's up to you. Start to notice any tenseness in your body and relax the muscles in those areas as necessary. Then check over again, more systematically this time, starting with the head – your eyes, face, jaw and mouth (open it a little); then down through your throat and neck, your shoulders, your arms, elbows and wrists, even your fingers. Notice all the places you never thought you could hold in tension, and let go. Continue down your back, chest, abdomen and stomach, letting each muscle group relax in turn; then your buttocks and groin area, descending eventually to your thighs, legs, knees, shins, calves, ankles and toes. Notice how it feels to be completely relaxed.

In your mind, go to a place where you feel peaceful and contented. Look at your surroundings and take in the pleasure they give you; notice the sights, the sounds and the smells. Use all your senses to bring yourself into that place. Become aware of how relaxed you feel inside, knowing the joy that lies deep within you because you are in this place. Be still and enjoy the moment.

When you are ready, gently begin to turn your thoughts to the events of today. As if watching a video recording, allow your mind to fast-forward through the day, showing you all that has gone on in the past few hours. Some thoughts will bring you pleasure, others may concern you. Pause only for a moment to acknowledge any concerns and put them on one side.

Turn your attention instead to one Moment of Treasured Joy that happened today. No matter how fleeting the moment, recall and re-live it. Take your time, and let your body and mind overflow with joy, just as it did earlier in the day.

And perhaps there are other moments of joy that you would wish to re-visit. Allow yourself to drift between these good times, refreshing the part of your mind that stores your joyful occasions. Take as long as you like to remember the pleasurable, positive events of your day, recognising how they have benefited your life and the lives of those you were with.

When you are ready, return to the present. You are back in your room feeling peaceful and relaxed – happy and contented as you come to the end of the day. Now, it is time to sleep.

## Visualisation for When You Feel Low

Sit or lie in a quiet place.

Identify how you are feeling – sad, lonely, unhappy, defeated, worried… Allow yourself to feel that way and accept that this is the way things are at the moment. Be gentle with yourself, because it's perfectly all right to be feeling like this.

Let your body relax.

Start at your head; tighten it and then let it go, feel your head relax.

Tighten your shoulders and neck, and then let them relax.

Go through each part of your body, tightening and relaxing.

You may need to repeat this if a particular part is very tense.

When your body is relaxed, allow yourself to release the thoughts going round in your head.

Imagine you are walking along a street; everything looks drab – grey buildings, concrete pavement – there are traffic noises and the smell of car fumes.

You walk along, feeling the way you are feeling now. You are not trying to change anything. You are just there, feeling low.

As you walk you notice, just ahead of you, something is pushing up through a crack in the pavement. You think it's probably only a weed, but it has a pretty flower. Then, you realise how incredible it is that something so small has managed to survive amidst all the concrete.

You take all this in and carry on walking, thinking about the tiny weed. It looked beautiful, bright green with little flowers. It must be really strong to have managed to get out into the air.

As you walk on, you find that your head is lifting. You notice that even though it's a grey day, there are different shades of grey, so that you can make out the shapes of the clouds. Some of them look familiar and you can almost imagine that one is a dragon or a whale. You find yourself beginning to pay more attention to your surroundings.

You walk past some small shops, hardly noticing what they are, but you can smell something good. You notice a bakery and you can see that an assistant is putting out a plate of freshly baked goods. You stop and look more closely and see your favourites on a tray in the window. You feel in your pocket, find some coins and go into the shop. You are even more aware of the wonderful aroma and you breathe in deeply and find yourself smiling as you make your purchase.

The assistant smiles back at you and your spirits begin to lift. You walk along biting into your treat, savouring the taste, totally aware of its delicious flavour. It brings back pleasant memories.

As you continue walking, a person who is coming towards you smiles and you find yourself responding and saying hello. At the end of the street you see a park and go in, feeling lighter in spirit.

You sit down on a bench and remember those brief moments you've just experienced that have made you feel so much better. You relax your body as you consider how different you feel and how you have changed by being aware of these small things – the weed coming through the pavement, the clouds with their strange shapes, the smell of the bakery, a smile, a pleasant place to sit down. When you feel like it, you get up and stretch. Then you walk home briskly, ready to get on with the rest of the day.

When you are ready, begin to come back to the present. Open your eyes and notice the change in how you are feeling. Slowly stretch and move each of your limbs. When you are ready, stand up. Look ahead of you and begin to get on with all the things you need to do.

## Acknowledgements

We thank all those who have contributed to the publication of this book:

John Adler of Pomegranate Books, for all your hard work, sharing your knowledge, support, guidance and good humour while producing the book. Beki for bringing out the essence of joy in your illustrations, and for your belief in the book and us; Adrian for sharing your expert musical gifts; Kate for photography and cheering us on; Mhairi, Colin and Gordon for your advice and help in enabling us to continue working during our visit to Iona; Andrew H, Brenda, Cora, Lavern and Suzy B for ideas and practical help; family, friends, members of our house group and healing group, for your interest and love.

The processes in Step 4, *Storing the Joy*, are inspired by material taught by John Seymour Associates Ltd, NLP Training and Consultancy, Bristol and London.

And finally, to our daughter Rachel and her fiancé Stuart, who were always on the end of a phone, encouraging us to keep moving ahead with the project.

Thank you all.

## About the Authors

 Alison taught young children for many years and now works as a Reiki healer and teacher. She loves family, friends, walking, reading, bird-watching and laughter. Her spirituality is enriched by her connections with the Quakers.

John spent most of his working life as an aerospace engineer. Nowadays, as a life coach and trainer, he helps people make the changes they wish for in their lives. He shares many of Alison's loves, and included in his TJ Moments are finding out how things work and mending them when they're broken.

Alison and John have been married for 20 years and live in Bristol.

Email: www.tjmoments.co.uk

## About the Illustrator

Rebecca is an artist with a passion for colour; her layering of paint creates luscious textures making her paintings a visual feast. Her work is collected and exhibited widely.

Her other passions include: campfires, buttons, poppy fields, thunderstorms and most of all having fun with family and friends.

She currently lives in Bristol with her husband Andrew and their children Mali and Blue.

Email: rebelines@hotmail.co.uk

## About the Book Consultant

 John left the University of Bristol, where he worked as a lecturer and arts adminstrator, to start his publishing imprint Pomegranate Books. Apart from his own publications, he spends much of his time helping authors to put their work into print, offering editorial, design and other services. He also works as a journalist, photographer and broadcaster, having produced a documentary for BBC Radio 4 in 2003.

John lives in Bristol and enjoys making furniture in his spare time.

Email: info@pomegranatebooks.co.uk